what she should have told a therapist to begin with

Emily Liberato

For Monahan.

Thank you for everything.
You deserve the world.
I hope a dedication is a good start.

what's ahead

thankful
help
alive

Keep at it.

Validity. I think that's something we all strive for. We want our stories to be valid in the eyes of others. We want our struggles and hardships to always have reasons behind them. We crave answers and that isn't necessarily a bad thing. At the same time, we also all know that too much of a craving can wreak havoc on our lives.

For too long I wanted for my feelings and reactions to always have reasons behind them. I could not accept the fact that this was just the way in which my brain has been hard wired, and sometimes a reason can't be created. Are the feelings and reactions valid? Of course. Do I always have control over how my brain and heart interact with and control each other? Absolutely not. That's why I initially started writing this book. If I couldn't find a reason behind the panic attack I was having, I decided to write about it. I decided to create something good out of something not so good.

But why, "she"? Why not, "I"? Initially, every poem was written in first person. This is my story, so I wanted to make it personal. As the stories continued, I came to the conclusion that I didn't want to associate myself so directly with the happenings in the poems. Not because I'm ashamed or embarrassed, but because I want to make sure others realize there's more to me than this mental fight I'm always battling. In addition, I wanted others to see themselves in my words. I'm sure as hell not the only one going through these exact situations.

No one deserves to feel alienated due to aspects in their life that they may never be able to change.

Everyone deserves a chance to be heard.

I guess this is what she, or what I, should have told a therapist to begin with.

The following poem is my first take on writing about mental health. "Numbers" was written about 3 years ago and I've been writing about mental health ever since. I'll continue to write about mental health for as long as I continue writing. We all have mental health. We all need to put attention and energy into it.

A stranger asks, "Oh what a precious
baby, how big is she?"
"21 inches, 7 pounds, 8 ounces"
But this stranger just had a child as well;
22 inches, 7 pounds, 9 ounces

It's your child's middle school
graduation.
You sit next to a parent who proclaims
their child plays four instruments.
You didn't ask, you don't even know
them, but they feel compelled to share.
Unfortunately, your dear child only
plays three.

It's her first day of high school.
She comes home stressed out of her
mind.
They had an assembly with the
freshman: grades, GPAs, and community
service hours,

as if college starts tomorrow for your
fourteen year old.

It's prom season and she's looking for
the perfect dress.
You hear concealed sniffles and as a
parent, you know what's wrong.
Your darling child is crying on the floor,
obsessing over sizes.
She can't find the perfect dress because,
"Mom, I'm just not skinny enough".

It's her senior year and she's attending
the pep rally.
The photos she takes will surface
eventually around 7:30.
"That's when everyone is on, mom".
But in a day the perfect shot is deleted
because, "it just didn't get enough likes".

You notice her friends are slowly
disappearing.
Her grades are dropping.
Her boyfriend has moved on to another.
She's not picking up her phone.

About a hundred gather.
Mass at ten, service at two.
You wish you could see your perfect
child one last time,
but six feet of dirt is now in the way.

senses

The attack hits hard.
Sometimes out of nowhere:
always uninvited,
always bringing a plus one
or two,
three,
four,
five,
as if she can sense she wants more;

as if it can sense that she doesn't want to
be alone.
She doesn't want to face the attach
without help,
without guidance to safety,

without a warning to others,

without a way to escape,

without a chance to see its destruction:
hear its taunting,
smell its vengeance,

taste its bitterness,
feel its power.

Her eyes scan the room,
looking for judgements.

Creating judgements.

They avoid those of spectators,
ensuring contact is never made
for the fear of being feared;

the fear of concerning to many too
aggressively,
the fear of drawing more attention
to a scene that is overflowing with
illustrations of panic.

They see the panic.
She sees the stares.

She sees the confusion.

She sees herself --
of what used to be.

Whispers begin,
or so she thinks.

She can barely hear over her own
thoughts,
filling her mind of nonsense.

But it's too powerful.

She hears the clock ticking by.

Time passes slower in these moments
as she stands there
begging someone for help.

But no one hears her ear-piercing yells
as she has fallen silent,
forgetting how to voice her pleads,

forgetting how to ask for help,

forgetting the power held behind her
voice.

She has been stripped,
left alone with her thoughts without
escape.

Memories flood her mind,
of better times
as her sense of smell strengthens
to remind her
there are better times.

There's the salt of the ocean waiting to
welcome her;
the unmistaken stench of nail polish
waiting to replace her freshly chipped
coat;
the fresh aroma of bread waiting at
home to fill her nauseated stomach.

But in this moment, she is reminded of
the smells that will forever haunt her.

Expo markers will always send her into
a mild panic
followed by the smell of the cleanser
that removes every word she must
remember.

It's hard for her to forget
the sense that is so often the strongest:
the sense that brings instant joy,
the sense that brings instant fear,
the sense that forces her to succumb to

word vomit --
lessening her of her grasp on reality.

Any words that manage to escape
taste stale and bitter:

not easy to release
for they try to come back down.

Tasting like
regret
and embarrassment
and fear
and sorrow.

Sorrow tastes the worst
as it combines everything
and everyone
into a stew of emotions
and worries
and disappointments and

everything.

She strives
to be grounded.

She desperately wants to feel the people
around her.

She wants to feel the floor,
walls,
chairs,
tables,

to ensure it's all real.

It's happening
and she can't stop it.

She feels her world crashing beside her
and in front of her
and above her
and behind her
and below her.

Everything she felt she had a handle on

is now slipping from her sweat filled
hands as she tries to regain sense;
as she tries to regain all her senses

for they have drained her
of her power.

debts

Not a day goes by
where her mind isn't flooded with all
that she owes:
who she needs to speak with
and who she needs to reconcile with
and who she needs to come clean to.

To speak would be to mention.
To reconcile would be to apologize,

but for what?

To come clean would be to radiate truth
like never before

as if her life depended on it,

as if the truth will set her free.

But getting to the truth isn't easy
as her mind distracts her from it.

Without truth

she will continue to suffer
and continue to cry out for help, silently
and continue to lose hope
and continue to owe.

Everyone wants her to speak.
They sense a disturbance

but she's afraid if she starts,
she won't stop.

A disturbance.
A burden.

Herself: a burden.

For she does not, cannot, see what
others see.

They see someone who needs help.
She sees someone who's overreacting.

They see someone who can't do it alone.
She sees someone who deserves to be
alone because she hurt them too much
by speaking too much

even though not a raw word has left her mouth.

Not a raw word has left the lips that have been torn to shreds.
Not a raw word has left the throat that dries up from sobbing spells.

Not a raw word has left the teeth that grind in fear.

Not a raw word has left the girl who desperately needs to be heard.

Instead, her words are overdone, garnished, served up to look perfect.

There's no need for her to continuously apologize
but she can't help it.

Of course she can --
but she won't.

Not until every last person she has
wronged has been addressed:
every time she sees them
every time she thinks about them
every time they are mentioned.

As if not apologizing with every interaction
will allow for grudges to be made.

Grudges aren't allowed.

Because grudges mean confrontation.
Confrontation invites an attack.

Not from them

but from the beast
that pleads at her to repeat every
apology
until she memorizes them;
she won't miss a beat,
so the attack won't kill her,
only wound her enough to continue
with more strength.

Picture this:
she's running a race
against the beast
and by coming clean
it gets her ahead.

But the beast doesn't want this,
can't stomach this,
so it gets a second wind

and wins.

Losing to the beast
is her biggest fear.

Coming clean
makes her address her biggest fear:
addressing all it has done,
all is has ruined,
all it has stolen.

Coming clean shines light onto the
darkest part of her life:

illuminating the countless hours of lost
sleep,
the days spent laying in bed, afraid to
face the world,
the school hours spent avoiding classes,
the swollen eyes,

the swollen eyes that take in every
attack,
the swollen eyes that see the damage
done every day,
the swollen eyes that see those around
her, not affected,
the swollen eyes belonging to the girl
who wants to defeat it,
and reclaim the large, brown eyes once
full of hope.

excuses

She's sorry.

She's sorry she's crippled
with the breath-taking diagnosis.

She can't breathe
and she can't muster up the strength to
say anything but

sorry.

School messes with her mind
like nothing else.
It has the power to make her feel full of
hope and joy
and yet has the power to strip that from
her in a matter of seconds.

The dreaded presentations,
the weight of group projects,
the simple task of passing her
classmates as she goes to hand in a piece
of paper

are all too much.

Presentations are packed full of piercing
eyes of peers.
Group projects include overcritical
glares giving her a great deal of
goosebumps.
Handing in assignments hazards harsh
hazes and hateful heckling --

or so she believes.

Deep down she knows this to not be the
case.
She knows this to be a picture drawn up
by her brain
in which her heart so painstakingly
colors in

perfectly,
because even her distorted reality must
be just that:

perfect.

She had always been the kid who
teachers fawned over:
the kid who had the "it" factor,
the kid who had potential,

who had\never met the beast..

At the tender age of 8, her life was
golden.

At the tender age of 18, her life was
being thrown into the firing pits of hell

as she watched those whom she loved,
leave her,
as she watched years of hard work be
shoved down the drain
and washed away with the rest of her
dreams,
 as she watched her world become a
world without potential:

a world where the beast has emptied the
once overfilled bucket of opportunities
and
brightness she, and everyone around
her, once thought was larger than life.

At the tender age of 18, her big brown
eyes had trouble seeing a future with
the potential
she once ravished in.

Maybe at the tender age of 8 her golden
life was already beginning to tarnish.

Her golden state was a facade for her
life happenings.

At the tender age of 8, she was forced to
lose one after the other.

At the tender age of 8 she learned that
maybe the next phone calls her mother
got
were of funeral times.
At the tender age of 9, she got to
continue living this nightmare.

One
after the other
after the other
after the other
after the other
after the other.

Until she had witnessed death and
sorrow for almost every one year she
herself had been
alive.

At the tender age of 19, she understands.

She understands where it all stems from

She understands where it all manifests.

She understands where the beast was
born from.

She understands it's not her fault.

But she's sorry.

Every night she lays in bed
hoping to hear from her beloved
friends:
the ones that support her
and care for her
and want to see her happy.

Most nights she's wanted:
wanted to be in attendance of a simple
hangout
with one
or two
or three
good, great, amazing
friends.

Some nights she gets an invite
to an event that should be fun
an event that should kick off a great
weekend
an event that should make anyone want
to get up and get ready for it 5 hours
before.

But every night
she lays there in bed
as she knows no one invited the beast.
No one invited the piece of her she can't
get rid of.
No one invited all of her.
They simply invited the body that
houses what used to be of her;

the body that fights the beast every
night.

And she knows her friends mean well --
they always have and they always will.

She's told them about the beast,
she's told them details.

But only details she can muster up the
strength to admit,
only details the beast accidentally
allows to slip out of her mouth.

To her friends

she's sorry she declines more than she
accepts,
she's sorry she would rather be alone.

But please don't mistake that as wanting
to feel alone.

Sure, she has the company of the beast
every night,
sure, that fills a void that may be
dangerous if left unfilled.
But she doesn't want to feel alone.

Invite her,
expect a decline,
but invite her.

She's sorry.

reoccurrences

As she walks home
she notices a car pulled over.

This is it.
This is where she'll face death head on.

A moment passes and the car drives off.
The moment passes, but the thoughts
remain.

She passes a group of people, talking
amongst themselves.
Of course they're talking about her.
There's no other reason why they would
be laughing.
She must have had something in her
hair.

A moment passes and the group is heard
down the street, laughing amongst
themselves.
The moment passes, but the thoughts
remain.

She arrives home, fumbles with her
keys, and can only muster one thought.
Someone has a perfect chance to take
her or hurt her or kill her.

A moment passes and she gets inside
safe. Heart racing, but safe.
The moment passes, but the thoughts
remain.

She knows no one is out to get her
and no one is talking about her
and no one is waiting for her.

Her immediate physical world seems
too perfect.

This can't be all there is.

rehearsing

It's not uncommon
for her to have something to contribute
that she will rehearse before speaking.

But by the time the perfect opportunity
comes for her to speak
she misses it.

Because she's too busy perfecting what
she'll say
that she's tuned out.

Her energy is a selfish energy.

She worries so much about her own
composure
that she fails to truly listen to those
around her.

And when she does pay attention
her energy is nonexistent,

for she has given up on even the idea of
contributing

in fear of making a fool of herself
in fear of being incorrect
in fear of imprinting those around her
with a negative outlook on who she is

and who she secretly houses.

She wonders to herself:
"what if"?

What if the response that came out of
her quivering mouth is misconstrued as
a sly remark
as she hasn't had a chance to fully catch
her breath?

What if the simple act of asking a
question makes her seem incapable of
the simplest tasks?

What if she's viewed as someone less,
because she's carrying more?

She's carrying another being, and it
takes over every ounce of energy she
has.

What if she can't succeed because of
her, "what ifs"?

What if she wasn't plagued with the
draining mass that is the beast?

What if
she were born
alone.
Alone is what she wants to be.

She doesn't want to constantly drag this
mass who destroys all joy
and all happiness
and all feeling of success
and all --

What if?

Night has never been a safe place for
her.
It's full of a dark abyss where her mind
fills the void;
filling it with images of monsters of both
the physical and mental caliber,
filling it with shadows casted from dim
lights illuminating from outside
where the quiet world is suddenly
amplified.

Every noise louder than the one before.
Every noise belonging to a world she
has not yet figured out.

Tonight, she lays in bed early.
It's been a good day, a great day--

a day to remember.

A tired body takes its place in her bed.
But a restless mind takes over.

Tossing and turning until four hours
have passed.
At this point she has awoken the beast..

And while she thought she was ending
the perfect day with a good night's sleep,
she becomes suddenly aware that isn't
the case.

Why would it be?

The beast was disguised.
It was just waiting for the perfect
moment
to ruin her perfect day.

Tonight, the void becomes a space for
thoughts to run ramped;
hours of uninterrupted darkness are
ready to be filled.
She shakes as panic seeps deep within
her.

She breathes uneasily as her thoughts
become ones she cannot stop.

She rocks back and forth, waiting for the
attack to be over,
waiting for the beast to become as tired
as she is,
waiting for her physical state of being to
override her mental state.

But she knows this to not be an easy
task.

For she knows the beast has been
waiting all day.
It was waiting for the perfect time to
strike.
Every night seems like a perfect time
for no one is awake to hear her silent,
piercing cries.

But tonight's different.
No one expects this tonight.

It was too good of a day
for it to all of a sudden be taken over.

Too bad no one's awake to say
goodnight.

triggers

She was once full of confidence
and a charismatic outlook towards her
days to come
but that all changed
once presenting cursed her of ever
finding the positives in everyday life.

Formal presentations make her heart
race at the speed of light,
cause her hands to shake like she's
trying to rid herself of a never-ending
fire that has encapsulated her
extremities,
and cause her body to numb as if she
has been stuck, frozen in ice,
waiting for someone to come thaw her.

The most daunting presentation is life
itself.

It's a New England winter,
yet she refuses to bundle up
in fear she'll look too big.

She'd rather freeze than feel the eyes of
an innocent stranger as she passes by.

But who cares?
It's winter.
Everyone's bundled up.
No one wants to freeze.

But not everyone lives with a beast..

Not everyone has that sought-after
constant company.
Not everyone is made to think the worst
of themselves.

But she can't help it.
She can't help but believe the thoughts
racing through her mind.

They're too loud.

They're being screamed out,
in hopes of being heard.

In hopes of being validated.

She recognizes the volume.

She listens.

She stares in the mirror,
puts on her sweater,
walks out the door,

and freezes.

There is no where she'd rather be
than exactly where everyone else
believes she should be.

She can't disappoint others
like how she disappoints herself.

Expectations run ramped
and make her feel small,
like a minute detail in an acclaimed
novel.

Everyone is succeeding
and chasing their dreams
and following their hearts
and making themselves proud.

She's lowering her expectations for
herself
because
if they're low enough
she'll feel good.

She'll feel the pride she so badly misses.
She'll feel the pride she once had so
much of.
She'll feel the pride that is usually being
worn by the beast.
The beast's proud.

She's sorry.

mind

Her mind houses
hours
and days
and weeks
of thoughts she can't even begin to
express.

Her thoughts have thoughts of their
own,
making her head so full

of hypotheticals,
personal judgements,
and questions.

She questions all that can.
She questions why her mind is such a
mess.
She questions why her heart is so full
for everyone but herself.
She questions when it will all change,

because right now,

her mind is too crowded.

Her mind needs one less occupant.

The beast needs to be evicted for the sake of everyone.

For the sake of her sanity.

If she loses what's left of her sanity, the beast wins.

She can't afford to lose anymore.

Silencing her thoughts
sounds simple

until it isn't.

Silencing her thoughts
requires energy she's been drained of;

energy that's been long gone,
never to be felt again.

The beast uses stealth.
It knows her mind is the easiest place to
manipulate.

The louder the beast is,
the more silent she grows

as she's afraid if she speaks,
her words will inevitably become
overpowered.

Her thoughts are so deafening,

that she has trouble listening to those around her.

She can't see the girl they all swear is making progress

because all she sees is the girl the beast describes to her.

She can only see the girl who's constantly failing and falling behind in this life

because her thoughts are so ear piercing that she's become a stranger

living in this body

driven by the beast

who has no remorse.

Even a mere moment spent in her mind
would drive anyone up a wall.

Everything
must be even

because everything
must feel even.

So much of the energy she has left
is spent on making her outside world
appear as a utopia
compared to
the dystopia
going on within.

She lives her life
in order to feed the beast;
it's starving.

She lives her life
not for her.

If she lived her life for her,
she wouldn't allow herself
to get drenched in the rain
because she grabbed the wrong
umbrella,
and God forbid if her umbrella
doesn't match
her outfit.

If she lived her life for her,
she wouldn't care
if her ice
in her ice water
has melted,
because God forbid if the waters,
don't match.

If she lived her life for her,
she wouldn't care.

She wouldn't notice such minute details
if she weren't living to keep up the
facade
that her outside world
mimics her inside,

being ruled by a tyrant.

identity

She's afraid she'll never amount
to the girl she once thought she could
be.

She's afraid she loves too hard,
too quick,
as she's afraid she'll lose it all in a
matter of seconds.

She's afraid she'll never be loved,
truly and utterly loved,
by someone who hasn't known her long
enough,
for the beast is too aggressive.

The beast makes her believe she's
unlovable,

unwanted.

She'll believe this until she's proven
otherwise.

Until then,
she'll stay silent.

She'll stay silent,
not because she wants to,
but because she needs to.
One slip and there they go.
One slip and she's back to square one.
One slip and she's defeated.

The beast wins.

She's scared --
petrified.

Who she has become
is someone she often doesn't recognize:

someone who has been worn down
to the bone,
to every nerve,
until she has become something of a
different entity.

Reflections show a teenage girl, draped
with brown hair, freckles plastered
along the fair skin nestled snugly below
her big brown eyes.

But she sees a girl with ever changing
hair for every time she panics, she takes
it out on
what frames her face.

A girl whose freckles sit upon greying
skin that has been stripped of the
wonders of sleep

for she has spent sleepless nights
picturing a new reflection;
one that isn't being attacked.

She sees a girl whose once, big brown
eyes, held a dream and a want for a
bright future
but are now sunken in with visions of
stark reality that she can't figure out
how to change.

This is what she sees.

But she knows it's not her.

Who she has become
is someone she often doesn't recognize:

someone who has been worn down
to the bone,
to every nerve,
until she has become something of a
different entity.

Reflections show a teenage girl, draped
with brown hair, freckles plastered
along the fair skin nestled snugly below
her big brown eyes.

But she sees a girl with ever changing
hair that represents key moments in her
life.

A girl whose freckles sit upon greying
skin that has been stripped of the
wonders of sleep

for she has spent sleepless nights
excited for upcoming days planned to be
as magical as
can be.

She sees a girl whose once, big brown
eyes, held a dream and a want for a
bright future
but are now sunken in with visions of
reality that she is using every day to try
and figure out.
Because she knows she can't change her
life in a single moment.
She knows it takes time.

This is what she sees.

It's her.

strength

The beast and her are one in the same
in a very unfortunate, yet fortunate
sense.

For she is full of flaws --
as the beast points them out every time
she sees her reflection,
every time she meets someone new,
every time she's around anyone.

But the beast has flaws.

The beast isn't as strong as once
believed
for it gives her more power.

It gives her the power to see less flaws
in those around her.

It gives her the ability to stray away
from judgmental thoughts

about everyone,

but herself.

The beast will never let her go a day
without a judgmental remark to entice
tears,

but the only tears streaming come from
her eyes
as she dares not to ever make someone
else feel the pain of the beast..

Not through herself:
she will not allow the beast to slip in
that way.

This strips the it of its power.

It will always have a hold on her life

but it makes her a better person

because she knows the pain of living
with a beast

and wouldn't wish it on her worst
enemy.

She's sorry she's put everyone through
the wringer.
She's sorry she allowed it to get as bad
as it did.
She's sorry she may never have
complete control.

She's sorry she'll be forever needing
help,

but she's thankful.

She's thankful for the life she lives.

She's thankful for the attention the beast
is receiving.

Believe it or not,
the beast is shy--
it doesn't do well in the limelight.

Spending more time discussing the beast

and less time succumbing to its
destruction

will make it that much more unlikely to
return
and that much more unlikely
to wreak havoc
on the life
she's trying to build up
and live

on her own.

She has realized for a while now
that progress will not be made
without a little help:

help from family who just want what's
best for her,
help from friends who have been where
she is,
help from professionals who know how
to handle the beast with grace,
help from meds that help silence the
beast.

She needs help
to take away its destruction,
and its taunting,
and its vengeance,
and its bitterness.

Most importantly
the help takes away its power.

Without its power

it feels helpless.

It can't hurt her anymore.

She has anxiety,
and battles depression,

and that's okay.

She recognizes her health issues
and tries her hardest to have good days,
but often fails,

and that's okay.

She's an advocate for mental health,
and urges those around her to put their
own mental health first,
but often doesn't listen to her own
advice

and that's okay.

She's learning.
She's growing.

Admitting her

raw,
untainted,
and unearthed mental health issues
leaves her feeling vulnerable.

But she's not afraid anymore.

She's not afraid of the beast.
She's not afraid of the outcome of her
advocacy.
She's not afraid to demand change.

She's trying.

She's surviving,
and,
most importantly,

she's finally living.

Made in the USA
Middletown, DE
20 January 2019